Your Dating needs Updating

-You wanna get married don't cha?

By

Theresa Leneta Hall

Your Dating needs Updating

ISBN-13: 978-1721842070

ISBN-10: 1721842071

Thank You

I would like to take the time to thank all of my biggest supporters for always being there to give me the extra push I needed to follow my life-long dreams. You all encouraged me to never give up on who and what I wished to be or on the accomplishments that I aspired to achieve. It takes a village to raise a child and I am grateful for my village.

To my husband-thank you for always encouraging me in writing and beyond. You have been my knight in shining armor since the day we met. I know that God joined us to show others that real love does still exist. I pray that God continues to keep us safe in his arms as we grow and prosper together.

To my mom-you never cease to amaze me. Your nurturing, sincere, kind spirit is what I admire the most. Everyone who is graced with your presence feels the angelic soul that you are. I am forever grateful to you for your wisdom and guidance. I could never repay you for the love you've given me and honesty you've shown me since birth, but I hope that I've made you proud thus far. I love you!

To my daughter-I don't believe you know this, but you have been my biggest motivator since the moment I knew you were coming into this world. You are by far the best and most precious gift I have ever received in life. Please follow your dreams and know that your mom will always support you in whatever you wish to do. I cannot adequately express how proud I am of you and I know that you will keep moving on to bigger and better things. Thank you for actually listening to your mom and trusting me with your care. I love you forever and always because you are half of me and I am half of you.

Also, thank you to all who supported me by purchasing this book. I hope that it helps you in some shape, form or fashion. I can't express how much it means to me that you have entrusted me with your listening ear. God bless you!

Table of Contents

Introduction

Sometimes, we rush to do what we feel we are ready for when in actuality, we are not prepared to handle all that a situation entails. Marriage is a serious, life-long commitment that requires lots of attention, patience and compromise. It is like no other experience that you will have in life. Therefore, when a woman decides that she is ready to settle down, she should consider all things, not simply the idea of marriage. You see, you could marry just about anybody these days, but that's not what you want to do. You want to marry your soul mate or your best friend. You want to marry someone who will stick with you through the good times and the bad ones; someone who will make you laugh when you're feeling down or hold you to comfort you. Marriage can be a beautiful thing with the right person, but a storm with the wrong one. This book was written for women who wish to successfully date with the ultimate goal of that dating leading to a successful marriage.

Chapter 1

Love Yourself First

Every woman will eventually ask herself this question: "Why am I still single?" Women want to be loved, pampered and claimed by someone. Without these things, we feel incomplete. But how can we believe that we are ready for love when we are not one hundred percent in love with ourselves? Therefore, I would say that the first step to preparing for a mate would be to love yourself first. This means that you should focus on becoming happy with who you are. If you are not happy with your weight, do something about it. If you are not content with your career, take steps to bettering the path that you're on or switch to a new one. Anything you can do or have wanted to do, DO IT! Improving one's life whether physically, financially, spiritually or in any other way is always a good idea. I've never heard anyone say that they regretted changing their life for the better. It is ultimately an investment in you that can only be profitable.

Loving yourself also means keeping yourself up. Maintain your hair, nails and body. Purchase clothes that fit properly. Treat your body to a massage every now and then. We all need a break from working, taking care of others, and from the overall hustle and bustle of our everyday lives. Finding a mate is much easier when you feel good about yourself.

Another part of taking care of yourself means going to the doctor and to the dentist regularly. It is easy to take health for granted when everything seems to be going well and working properly. However, your health should be number one on your priority list at all times. Preventative health maintenance is the key to making sure that you live a long well-preserved life.

Another remedy that goes along with taking preventative measures is exercising. Visit a gym as often as you can or take a jog in the park. I like to mix my workouts up and find classes or exercise DVDs that I enjoy. This way, I never become bored and it's harder for me to come up with an excuse for not working out.

Along with everything else mentioned, loving yourself also means taking care of your mental stability. The mental is essentially more important than the physical. You should work on yourself from the inside out. What is on the inside will shine through to the outside. Sometimes, our emotions get the best of us and we lose control. Therefore, whenever you feel that you are not in control of yourself or your actions, you should seek outside counsel. This could be from a close family member or friend, but I would recommend that you explore professional help instead. Most of the time, we simply need to vent to someone without fearing judgement. A professional counselor does just that and can also refer you to other programs or groups that could assist you in the future. They can also prescribe medications that help you maintain control. We often do not think of seeking help because there is a negative stigma around doing so, yet there is never anything wrong with taking care of yourself in such a manner. We all need a mental tune-up every now and then.

Occasionally, one does not need professional help when their psychological health is thrown off. A day off of work, a vacation or sleeping in does the trick. If any of these work, then you were probably tired and just needed a break. I think adults should get mental health days from work like kids get weather days or teacher work days off from school. Employees would be much happier and more productive. I use paid time off from my employer whenever I need time to myself.

Society

After we have taken care of ourselves, sometimes it is still hard for us to feel good about ourselves since society has convinced us that all women should be Barbie doll perfect. That if we do not fit this image, we are not beautiful. This is why some women have multiple surgeries on various areas of their bodies and inject themselves with chemicals to appear young forever. Why would you re-paint a masterpiece that was already painted by the creator himself? Your physical appearance was not a mistake. Natural beauty is the best beauty you can possess and it doesn't cost a thing. Fall in love with yourself each time you look in the mirror. Do not get caught up in what society deems beautiful. Beauty does not stop at physical appearance. It can be in how you carry yourself, speak and treat others and in all of your other attractive characteristics. There is someone who is going to love you just the way you are.

At last, loving yourself does not mean that you are self-centered. It means that you are about yourself so much that you will not accept foolishness in your life. It means that you will stay away from negativity and only allow positive energy around you. It means that you will do whatever it takes to improve your life and that you are willing to allow others who wish to be included in those things to come around. We accept the love that we think we deserve. If you think you should be treated like a queen, then that is what you will require. If you have low self-esteem, then you will accept much less. If you do not love yourself before trying to love someone else, you will put someone else's needs and wants before your own in a relationship. This could be a huge mistake.

Worksheet

1. Am I current on my annual doctor/dental appointment?

2. How is my mental health? Do I need to see a counselor? Why or why not?

3. Am I happy with my physical appearance? What are some things that I would like to work on?

4. How many activities do I participate in to get my heart rate up? Is that enough? What are some activities/workouts that I would like to try?

5. Is there anyone/anything causing negativity in my life? If yes, what do I need to do to resolve it?

Chapter 2

Do Not Stress

Do not stress about finding a mate. If you do, you will date any man that comes your way. Even if you know what your standards are, you will settle and make excuses for dating him. I know that your biological clock is ticking and that your mom keeps saying that she wants grandkids, but you want to ensure that he is a good quality man who will stick around for an extended period of time before you start thinking about all of that. And just because he's a good quality man, that does not mean that he is ready for or even wants to be in a committed relationship with you. Get to know a man as a friend before you start a relationship with him. We all could avoid a lot of heartache and pain by simply taking things a little slower and getting to know one another first. You may find that he is just not right for you or vice versa early on in your "getting to know each other" investigation. Rushing to do something usually ends poorly. How many times have you rushed out of the house and forgot an item, left your curling iron on or forgot to arm the alarm? How many times have you been rushing to get to work, driving like a bat out of hell, and were almost in a car accident? We rush to do things because we believe that we do not have much time. Reprogram your mind to believe that you have all the time in the world and you will not stress about finding your mate.

One way to free yourself of stressing to find a mate is to fill your life with hobbies that you enjoy. I like to write, so every time I feel like I don't have anything to do, that is how I occupy my time. You may like to exercise, read, work in the garden, make jewelry or bake cookies. Whatever you enjoy, spend your time doing it. It could be two or three things. Just keep busy so that you do not sulk about being single. Singledom is not supposed to be depressing. Being single should introduce you to what works for you in potential partners and what does not. If you execute the dating rules properly, you will gather some vital information that will lead to your desired destination.

If you cannot think of things that you like to do at home, volunteer at one of your local charities, homeless shelters or organizations. I bet that you will find this rewarding and the people with whom you work will surely appreciate your time. There is nothing more fulfilling than to see a child's face light up as you read to them at a local library or the smiles and laughs you receive from a senior citizen as you take the time to talk to them. I'm sure there are dozens of organizations in your area that could use a helping hand. Look up a few and see which ones interest you or need the most help. There are plenty of things that you are able to teach a child or teenager because you were once in their shoes. Many young girls need positive role models to teach them etiquette, problem-solving skills, financial skills, etc. Sometimes, children do not come into contact with adults who are knowledgeable about these things and so they may never learn them. Your services are definitely needed in your community.

Still stressing? Well, if you are spiritual, make sure that you are a member of a local church. For some, this would be their first step in relieving stress. What do your spiritual beliefs say about relationships? I know that we all want to plan our own lives, but if you believe in a higher power, then maybe you should practice what your guide says. Hey, what do you have to lose? Nothing else has worked so far, right?

Stressing too much about anything could lead to an unhealthy situation. There are many side effects that can be caused by stress: headaches, chest pain, low energy, tense muscles, etc. I've even heard doctors assert that it could lead to a heart attack! No one wants any of those problems so proactively maintain your stress levels on a daily basis.

Stress Relievers

- Exercise

- Hot bubble baths

- Meditation

- Attending a religious service

- Rest and relaxation

- Vacations

- Aromatherapy

- Talking to a non-judgmental source

- Laughing

- Deep breathing

- Social Interaction

- Journaling

- Listening to soothing music

- Walking

Chapter 3

Surround Yourself with Men!

Yes, you read that correctly. Surround yourself with men. This is the good part. Have as many male friends as you do female friends if not more! How else are you going to learn their habits, characteristics, hobbies and what they desire in a woman? Lots of people think that men and women cannot be friends. I beg to differ. However, there is a trick to it. You have to set boundaries in advance. Oftentimes, you know if you wish to pursue a relationship with a person right away. If you do, then take it slowly. If you do not, then immediately put him in the friend zone and stick to your guns so that no one gets hurt. Just because you are friends with a man does not mean that you should eventually date him or sleep with him.

Guys like to hang out with their platonic female friends sometimes. They want to know as much about us as we want to know about them. You cannot spend all of your time with your girlfriends thinking that they will tell you all that you need to know about men. Your girlfriends can give you pointers and advice, but how do you get a male's perspective without any males around? I love to ask my female friends and my male friends about a particular situation and see how different their answers are. It gives me balance and makes me understand that the male and female species think and act tremendously different.

How do I surround myself with men, you ask? You talk to guys at work, church, social events and at the grocery store. You exchange numbers with guys who pique your interest or who you believe have something to offer. Some exchanges will turn into dates, some will turn into friendships and others will turn into business contacts. Women are always looking for the best places to find men. I'm here to tell you that they are everywhere! If you only get out of the house for work and go back into your cave, then of course you will not run into many. Being single should mean being social. What else do you have to do with your time? I have a friend who swears that there are no men in her area, but after work, all she does is go home and watch TV. She does not strut her stuff at the gym, hang out with friends or even attend church. How is a guy supposed to find you when you are hidden at home? They do not know where you live and I am sure that you do not want strangers randomly knocking at your door anyway. Get out and mingle!

Places to meet attractive and eligible men

- Sports bars and restaurants

- Home improvement stores

- Hunting/fishing stores

- Military bases

- Gun shows

- Car shows

- Sporting events

- Breweries

- Music events

- Religious or spiritual institutions

- The gym

- Work

- Social Media

Chapter 4

Let the Men Chase You

Now that you have surrounded yourself with men, you should know that you should allow them to chase you. Men are natural predators. They like to hunt, so let them. We are intended to be the prey that they seek; the prize they are trying to win. It is an ego boost for them to know that they had to chase you to get you. If you chase them or are too easy, they lose interest rather quickly. Yes, some men like aggressive women, but most do not. If they are intrigued by you, then they will find a way to get to know you. They will ask for your number or add you on Facebook or look at your badge while you are on the elevator at work and email you (this actually happened to me). It is fairly simple to communicate these days. If a guy is seriously interested or even a little interested, he will be sure to contact you one way or another. No job or event will keep him from at least sending you a message. It only takes a minute and he will most likely do it from the cell phone that he carries around for the majority of the day.

It is ok to flirt with a man, go up to a man and start a conversation or involve yourself in something that a man is doing, but I suggest that you do not ask him for his number. Remember, he is the hunter, you are the prey. If he wants to get to know you, he will find a way. I know this is the 21st century and times have changed, but some things remain the same. Men are first visual creatures. They have to be physically attracted to you to even look your way. If they are not physically attracted to you, then there is no reason for you to try to win him over with your personality. So, if you wore your best tight pants, batted your pretty eyelashes, smiled, laughed and talked with him for ten minutes and he still did not bite, then he's probably already taken or simply not interested.

The Chase

Like I said before, men like to chase after what they want. If I had a dollar for every story I've heard about a man chasing a woman that he really wanted until he finally pinned her down, I'd be rich! Men know exactly what they want and they go after it. This is precisely how my husband and I began dating. He saw me and asked for my number and I blew him off several times for several months before even going out with him. I was career-focused at the time and was not looking to be tied down by a relationship. However, any inkling of time that he could get from me, he took. A year later, we were dating and seven months after that, he proposed. I said all of that to say, that a man recognizes what he wants and will go through hell and high water for his chance to get it. If he does not put forth any effort, he is not interested. That does not mean that you aren't attractive, that you are uninteresting or that something is wrong with you. That may simply mean that the two of you are not a match. By trying to force yourself on someone, you're opening yourself up to drawn-out disappointment. He may play around with you and accept all of the benefits of having you around, but that won't change the fact that you were never his type in the beginning. We meet people all the time who are not meant to be in our lives forever. One-time chance encounters are okay to have.

On the contrary, do not rush nature. Just because a guy does not ask for your contact information the first time you meet him, it does not mean that he won't at a later time. If you saw him at a place that you visit regularly, chances are that you will see him again. I am a firm believer in destiny. If you are meant to meet someone or be with someone, it will happen.

Chapter 5

Stop "Dating" Married or Unavailable men

Yeah, I said it! What are you going to do about it?! Dating men who are already involved in a committed relationship is a dead-end street and you know it. It very rarely leads to him leaving his woman for you and if he does, he is just going to handle your relationship in the same way that he handled his previous relationship. Stop lying to yourself saying that you are just friends with him. Women's feelings get tied up very quickly in particular situations and this is one of them. Time and time again, we allow ourselves to get swept away by our imagination which tells us that he will drop everything for us and give us the white picket fence, two kids and a dog. In reality, he only wants you for what you are giving him and you know exactly what that is. He does not want to marry you, but he will probably tell you that he does because he knows that is what you want to hear. Do not believe a man wants to marry you until he produces a ring, gives you a firm date and has a plan to pay for all of it.

I am fully aware that some women prefer dating married or unavailable men because they can play with them and send them back home. They can deal with him when they want or ignore him altogether. They can call on him when they need something, get what they want from him and be done with him for as long as they desire. This becomes old rather quickly. After a few months of this, we get tired of the same ol' thing. We want a man who can stay with us all day and all night; a man who can eat dinner with us and the kids. A man who will romance us and not just "wham, bam, thank ya ma'am" us. We want a man to call our own. Therefore, women should not date married or unavailable men no matter how desperate they get.

Married or unavailable men cheat with you because you let them-not because you are better, prettier or smarter than his current woman. When he gets bored at home or angry with his spouse/girlfriend, you are his getaway. Think about it. Every time you are with him, what does he say about his partner? All bad things, right? He never states why he stays though, huh? If he is so unhappy at home, why doesn't he just leave her and be happy with you? He gives you excuses for staying saying that he is staying because of the kids or that it is complicated. Make him explain what is so complicated about it and I bet you will still be confused at the end of the conversation. What does him staying have to do with the kids? Can't he take care of his kids without staying with the woman or does he just not want to pay child support? Child support laws stay in effect for eighteen years or more, so if you want to see if he will be with you after the kids are grown, then by all means, be my guest. Men these days are savvy. They will say anything to keep you in their corner. No man is going to say to you that you are his side chick and that is how it is always going to be. He knows a good quality woman will not stand for that for an extended period of time.

Don't waste time on guys who are already involved with someone else. You are setting yourself up for failure and could be missing out on Mr. Right because you are letting Mr. Right Now absorb your time. With everything in life, you want to win. A favorite quote of mine is "Winners never cheat, and cheaters never win"-unknown. You cannot be successful in finding a soul mate by stealing him from someone else. In society, it is against the law to steal and the punishment is jail time. I always think that stealing of any kind is wrong. You may not receive jail time for cheating with someone else's mate, but you surely will encounter heartache because of it. Wouldn't you feel better having someone who is rightfully yours anyway?

Let's talk about what Mr. Wrong cannot give you. He cannot give you his undivided attention. When his spouse texts or calls and he is with you, he has to put you on hold to answer. She is forever priority over you because he goes home to her. He can only give you a few minutes or hours per week, only talk to you when he is away from home or not with his mate and only see you when it is convenient for him.

Mr. Wrong cannot give you money. I am talking about money that will pay your big bills such as a mortgage and car note; not money that will fill up your gas tank once or twice. Unless he is a rich man, he cannot just take five hundred dollars out of his checking account and hand it to you without his better half questioning it. He cannot spend all of his extra money taking you out to eat or shopping. He probably cannot take you out at all for fear of being seen by someone who knows him or his significant other.

Mr. Wrong cannot give you a committed relationship. Duh, he's already in one. Like I said before, if he does leave his significant other for you, you will be number one temporarily and there will soon be another woman filling the number two position that you were once in. You cannot teach an old dog new tricks. Old dogs are set in their ways and resistant to change; they will not change unless they truly desire to. I know that is not what you wanted to hear, but somebody has to tell you the truth. It may as well be me.

Mr. Wrong cannot give you tons of things. Unconditional love, marriage, kids and stability are just a few of them. He is only out to fulfill his own selfish desires. What man wouldn't want more than one woman if he could have it? That is pure greed: Desiring more than one needs or deserves.

I've mostly been talking about married men and men in committed relationships, but there are other types of unavailable men; for example, single men who tell you they are not ready for a relationship, too busy with their career or just not the settling-down type are unavailable men as well. Why? Because they are advising you up front that they only want a casual relationship with you. Usually, they are either not attracted to you, don't see you as the marrying type or they believe that you have too much baggage for them. Either way, not many guys turn down hanging out with a pretty lady or better yet, having sex with one, but that's not going to make him fall in love with you. He will be hanging with you and searching for his wife at the same time.

Limiting Your Options

When women think of Mr. Right, they think of the stereotypical guy who is tall, dark and handsome. I am here to tell you that Mr. Right most likely will not come in that package for you. You may receive one of those physical attributes or maybe even two, but most likely, not all of the above. Why do we focus on what he will look like instead of focusing on his other distinguishing qualities? Will those features make him a good boyfriend, husband or father? What I want women to do is to broaden their dating criteria. A good deal of women limit their dating options by dreaming of the perfect man and trying to find him in this world. You will never find the perfect man, because perfect does not exist. You can, however, find the perfect man FOR YOU.

Finding the perfect man for you means dating guys that you would not normally date. Your dream guy may be tall, but you should also date guys who are not as tall or is the same height as you. Your dream guy may be older, but also date guys who are your age or a little younger. I always thought that guys who were older than me were more mature; I have found this to be untrue. Your dream guy may be dark-skinned, but date fair-skinned or light-skinned individuals. You may even want to date guys of a different ethnicity. Love does

24

not have to look like you expected. The bible talks about what love does, not what it looks like physically.

Now, I am not telling you not to have standards, but I am telling you not to overemphasize what is not important. Of course you have to be attracted to him in some way, but most importantly, you should consider him as an entire package. One important thing to consider when choosing a mate is his stability-this includes his mental health. Is he crazy? Does he say off-the-wall things or scare you by what he does? No one has time for craziness, so you may want to look for the signs. What kind of job does he have and how long has he had it? Does he hop from one job to another? Is he an entrepreneur? Check out his living situation. Does he live with his mom? Why? How long does he plan to be there? Is he homeless or does he hop around from place to place? Lastly, check to see if he has unnecessary drama in his life. Drama causes unnecessary stress. How stable he is affects how stable the two of you will be together.

Another thing to do when searching for a mate would be to notice his characteristics. Is he charismatic? Is he polite? Is he romantic? Or is he rude, selfish and uncaring? If a guy is most of what you want, then you may want to give him a chance. If he does not fall in line with your values and desires, then you should not squander away your time on him.

Worksheet

1. Am I dating Mr. Wrong?

2. What is my type? Have these type of men
    been good to/for me in past relationships?

3. Am I allowing men to waste my time when I
    could be doing something more productive?

4. Am I open to dating men who are usually
    not my type? Why or why not?

5. Have I dated men outside of my usual type
    before?

6. Does my current mate have overall stability?

Chapter 6

Accept that you have made mistakes and move on

I began dating at the age of fifteen. I am now thirty-seven years old. From then until now, I've made so many mistakes that I've lost count. I am not proud of them; however, I trust that they've helped mold me into the person that I am today. Making mistakes is inevitable. No one can prevent you from making them. The only thing that you can do is try to make good decisions for yourself and your life. There is no sense in dwelling on the past. A mistake is meant to teach you a lesson. Either you learn from it and never make that mistake again, or you keep repeating the vicious cycle. Your life is your choice. Personally, I do not like emotional pain, so I try to avoid it at all costs. The more you know, the more you grow. However, some mistakes are a blessing in disguise. It only took me getting pregnant at seventeen once to know that I did not want to have another child out of wedlock. I could not have imagined how much a baby would alter my life. At the time, I did not understand why I was one of the ones who had to go through what I was going through. Now I know that if it weren't for her, my life would have taken a wilder path. She is my blessing in disguise and now I cannot imagine life without her.

Making mistakes is the part of life that says, "Hey, you did something wrong. The role you played in the relationship was not carefully carried out and you messed up. However, it is not the end. There is always room for change and there is always time to start over." Starting over can be done within a relationship or by releasing yourself from one. Either way, new beginnings can constantly happen. Where would we be without change? How could there be any growth without switching up a few things in different areas of our lives? I've changed my appearance, jobs, boyfriends and plenty of other things in life as I've grown. It is an intricate part of maturity. You would not accept the same conditions or behavior as an adult that you did as a child/teenager. Your level of growth would not allow for it.

Some people repeatedly make the same mistakes. Why? Either because they didn't learn their lesson the first time or they simply do not care to progress. I am a quick learner because I hate wasting time, energy and resources on things or people that do not benefit me in the long run. Being productive in all areas of my life is my ultimate goal and it should be yours as well.

Chapter 7

The Dating Process

Well, we have moved on to the dating portion of the book. I am not a relationship guru, a talk show host or a psychologist, but I've dated enough to know what works and what does not. A lot of people take advice from people just because they are well known. I was raised in the Deep South and lived in the ghetto. I was raised by my mom and step-dad, but my step-dad passed away when I was eighteen years old. My only biological brother was in prison from the age of eighteen until twenty eight. So when it came time for me to seriously date, I had no male figure to give me guidance. My only way of deciding if something was a good relationship or a bad one was actually being in one or the other. And let me tell you, I've seen and done more in my lifetime than a lot of people have seen or done in theirs. I've dated professional men, hustlers, abusive men, momma's boys, etc; you name him, I've dated him. I even had a high school sweetheart like most women. I made dozens of mistakes along the way, but all of them taught me valuable lessons. Dating is a learning process. You learn who you are when you are with someone else, you learn the person you're dating and you learn if you are willing to spend an ample amount of time and energy on a relationship.

Dating should be an enjoyable experience to say the least. You get to meet as many guys as your schedule can handle and have them take you out to some of your favorite places-all while possibly gaining a friend. You laugh, talk, hang out and act like teenagers on the phone. You have someone to take to your friends' couples parties, family gatherings and maybe even a wedding or two. Gone are the days where you show up to every event alone. You also have someone who can possibly help you by changing your tire or light bulb or bringing you soup when you are sick. How awesome is that?!

When dating, do not feel pressured to move quickly. You hold all of the power. A guy is only going to do what you allow. If he is as interested in you as you are in him, he will be as patient as you want him to be. Go on several dates with a person for several months before demanding a title. Be friends for a while. Women tend to want to lock a man down right away because we are afraid someone else will snatch him up if we do not first. Take---It---all---Tortoise-and-the-Hare slow. The tortoise won in the end...why can't you?

Once you have decided to be monogamous, set rules. If you do not like him seeing, still doing things for or talking to his ex, let him know that those things are not okay with you. If you want respect on social media, talk to him about it. If you do not like his partying ways, say something. Communication is very necessary in order to build an effective relationship. Without it, no one knows what the other is feeling. Humans are not mind readers. Sometimes, I wish I had that super power, but I realize that it will never show up. Steve Harvey came up with something called the 90-day rule in his book *Act like a Lady, Think like a Man*. It is a rule that says not to sleep with a man for the first ninety days of dating. Sounds like a winner to me! Make sure he is worthy of you first. Your body is a temple. I Corinthians 6:19 NIV says "Do you not know that your bodies are temples of the Holy Spirit, who is in you, whom you have received from God? You are not your own; you were bought with a price. Therefore honor God with your bodies." Wow! What a powerful scripture.

Chapter 8

Investigate

So, you're dating this guy and everything he says sounds too good to be true? It may or may not be. People will only tell you so much upfront because they do not want to scare you off. When I was twenty-five years old, I was approached by a guy who told me that he was twenty-three. He was actually eighteen. If I had known his true age, I wouldn't have taken him seriously. We dated for two years and his age showed as time went on. The moral of the story is to do your own investigation. Do not believe everything you hear. If he says that he is twenty-three, make him show you some ID. If he says that he has a job, watch his actions to see if he is telling the truth. People who do not have jobs typically sleep in, can call and talk to you all day and never have any money. If he shows gay tendencies, watch who he hangs out with and ask your gay friends if they know anything about him. If he says he is not married, call him in the middle of the night-see if he answers, if his phone goes straight to voicemail or if he is whispering trying to talk to you. Be intellectual about your investigation. Do not allow your emotions to get the best of you.

Some guys will tell you the truth and nothing but the truth so help them God, but I have not run into one of those yet. If you have, he is a keeper for sure! Sometimes though, you just have to decipher what is true and what is not. After dating for a while, deciphering becomes easier. If you are not sure that you believe something he told you, then you probably need to investigate it if it is important to you. By no means am I saying that you need to investigate every word that comes out of his mouth. Surely, you do not have time for that. If he lies that much, then he is a compulsive liar and you need to get out while you can.

Investigation is important today for your own personal happiness and safety. The more you know about a person before dating him, the better. I'm not saying you should be paranoid, but it is better to be safe than sorry. I like to think of dating backwards of the judicial system; the person is guilty until proven innocent. Call me crazy, but it has worked for me. Like I stated before, people only tell you what they think you can handle at the time. They do not want to scare you off in the beginning. They may gradually let you in on some things as time passes, but if the things they reveal to you are deal breakers for you, then you just wasted valuable time. There is nothing that I hate wasting more than time. It can never be given back to you. Guys believe that if they make you fall in love with them before telling you all of their dirt, then they have a better chance of you staying with them. I believe that there may be some truth to that. However, if a woman really wants a certain man, she will stay no matter what his flaws are. Every woman has her own list of things that she will and will not put up with. Sometimes, we do not find out what those things are until we are put in that particular situation.

Investigating in the beginning saves valuable time and energy. If you knew that a guy broke up with his long-time girlfriend the previous day, but was attempting to talk to you the following day, would you date him? Or would you give him time to figure out if he really wants to move on? If you're smart, you wouldn't want to get in the middle of that until the man shows that he is completely done with the situation. Feelings do not subside overnight. People need time to process how and why they are feeling a certain way. You jumping in the middle only adds more chaos.

Chapter 9

Dating Do's

I want to give a few tips on things that you should do when you are dating. In chapter 10, I will advise you on what not to do. Both are for your benefit as well as for the benefit of your partner.

1. DO let him know what you expect from the relationship. If you wish to be casual friends, want to be friends with benefits or are ready for marriage, you should discuss this.

2. DO tell him the truth. I know this is difficult because we all want to look like an angel to the other person, but the truth usually comes out in the end anyway. Avoid telling lies because after telling enough of them, you will eventually get caught in one.

3. DO offer to pay for a date. It will make him feel as though you are not a gold digger. When you are at the restaurant and the waitress brings the check, reach into your purse as if you are about to pay. If he is a gentleman, he will not let you, but you win points for offering. Let him pay for most of

the dates, especially the first one, but you can pay for a few here and there too.

4. DO meet some of his friends and family. If a guy takes you around his friends and, even more importantly, around a lot of his family, he is really feeling you. Meeting who he hangs around could bring insight to the kind of person he is and how family-oriented he is. Pay close attention to how he treats his mom. This says a lot about a man. He is probably going to treat you the same way he treats her. On the other hand, he may be a momma's boy so watch out for that too if momma's boys aren't your type.

5. DO listen to what he tells you. If a man tells you that he is not ready for a relationship, believe him. Men are pretty simple. If they tell you something like this, it usually means just that. They want to keep their options open and are not ready for a committed relationship. Spending lots of time with him, playing house with him and sleeping with him will not change his mind. He will only be ready for a relationship when he decides that he is ready.

6. DO ask to visit his home instead of allowing him to only visit yours. Some men never allow women to visit because they are living with another woman. They will claim they have broken up with that woman, but they still live together for one reason or another. I do not advise that you get yourself involved in a situation like that.

7. DO ask that he plan dates for the two of you instead of allowing him to come over to "Netflix and chill" every time. Planning dates is something that he's going to have to put some thought into and the way he feels about you will usually play out in the type of date he plans.

8. DO ask a lot of questions. I'm not saying to give him the third degree on the first date, but ask him a lot of questions and truly listen to his answers. A lot can be revealed through simple and honest conversation.

9. DO pay attention to his habits. Whether he smokes, drinks, degrades women, etc.-what he does may not align with your beliefs. You will be better equipped at making your decision on what type of relationship you

wish to have or not to have with him if you take those habits into account.

10. DO attempt to figure out his intentions as soon as possible. You don't want to spend lots of time with a man who only wants you as a friend if you're ready for a relationship.

Chapter 10

Dating Don'ts

1. DO NOT let him meet your kids too early in the relationship. Kids do not want to see people walking into and out of your life, and you shouldn't want to introduce them to everybody. You need to learn all about a person before you feel secure enough to bring them around your children.

2. DO NOT play house. Whoa! I know I just stepped on some toes. Playing house means acting like his wife when you are not even close to receiving that title. Running errands for him, taking care of his children, cooking and/or cleaning his house; none of that is going to make him like you any more than he already does. It is okay to invite him over for dinner sometimes and plan play dates for the kids, but do not play house if you do not at least have the title of fiancé. If he has access to all of those things without any real commitment, then he has no motivation to give you more than the title of girlfriend. I know you have heard the expression "Why

buy the cow when you can get the milk for free?" This is what that expression means.

3. DO NOT let him continue to get away with things that are deal breakers for you. If he cheats on you and that is not okay with you, then there has to be a consequence. Stop letting him do you the same way over and over again. I promise that if you stop taking his phone calls, stop visiting and stop having sex with him, he will think about what he has done; if he truly cares for you, he will not repeat the same action. He will not want to lose you permanently.

4. DO NOT shack up. This one is similar to number two except this means that the two of you have decided to live together while being boyfriend and girlfriend. I have never believed in this particular process, but I did try it once and low and behold, it was a disaster. If you must live together, at least have the title of fiancé before doing so. If he buys a ring, combines your bank accounts and pays bills with you, then he is serious about taking your relationship to the next level.

5. DO NOT lose yourself in a relationship. Losing yourself in a relationship means that you have put someone else before yourself. In chapter one, we talked about loving yourself first. You should always put your well-being and your life before another person's-especially one who is not committed to you by marriage. Even then, you should assess the situation very carefully.

6. DO NOT sleep with him on the first date. Yeah, I know we are all grown and our bodies tell us one thing while our minds tell us another and he may still respect you after you sleep with him on the first night, but then the thrill is gone. Guys like to believe that there is gold at the end of the rainbow that they are chasing. If you give him the gold right away, there is no need for him to chase you. He will think that going forward he can get it on every date and that is not the impression you want to give him. Make him wine and dine you, treat you like a lady and get to know you a little better before you two become physical.

7. DO NOT try to change him into who you wish him to be. People are who they are and

can only change themselves. Women believe that nurturing, fussing and fighting will get a man to eventually change. This is an unrealistic expectation and a set-up for failure.

8. DO NOT be afraid to re-visit your friend-zone list. One of the guys you friend-zoned, may actually be the perfect mate for you. There are probably men on your friend-zone list who adore you, would take care of you and would treat you like the queen you are, but you can't get past the fact that he doesn't look like Denzel.

9. DO NOT believe that you will be single forever. Forever is such a strong word. You will only be single for life if that is what you choose. Everyone wants, deserves and is destined for love.

10. DO NOT allow your emotions to deafen your voice of reason. In the beginning, lead with your head instead of your heart. Allow a man to gain your trust and then open up your heart. This will prevent a lot of heartbreak.

Those were just a few rules that I thought of off the top of my head. I will give you more tips later on in the book.

Chapter 11

The Downside of Dating

Dating is not always fun, easy or exciting. Realistically, you will be hurt several times before meeting your soul mate. You can avoid some of the heartache by choosing your partners wisely, investigating and taking things extremely slowly. I know it seems like a long process, but I promise that once you are hooked up with the right individual, everything else moves much faster. I believe that this is where being equally yoked applies. Your heart and soul ties are extremely important, so be thoroughly selective about who you allow to occupy your space.

Some guys play games and that is all they intend to do until they are ready to settle down or until they mature. These are the type of guys, with whom you dare not waste your time. They will use you, abuse you and never commit to you. They are just down right dirty in how they treat women and will play you until the end. My advice to you is to RUN! RUN! RUN!

Not every individual is deserving of your time so it is okay to be stingy with whom you share your days. A man who wants to be a huge part of your life will show you that. If he only wants to play games, you should call him out on it. Do not feel obligated to go out with someone or take their phone calls just because it's what they want. If you are not interested, tell him. You will waste enough time going out with guys that you do like; no need wasting time with guys that you don't.

Sometimes, you will meet men who you actually enjoy being around, but have found that you two are better off as friends. Bummer. That is okay. Men are good friends because they usually don't sugarcoat things when you ask for their advice and they are pretty fun to hang out with too. When you go out with them, they are super protective and will often buy you drinks all night because they like to feel important. Having cool male friends is a win.

You have to treat dating like a game of chess. There are two players. He'll make a move then you will, him then you and so on and so forth. Make sure your moves are strategic and in line with the end game you have in mind.

Chapter 12

Be Careful

As women, we have to be careful when dating. Every person does not have good intentions. There is evil in this world. I'm sure there is more evil today than ever before. You will encounter a few jerks, guys who want to take advantage of you for the things that you have and guys who just want to add you to their list of women. We are strong individuals and we need to be aware of what is going on in our lives at all times. This goes back to Chapter eight where I say to investigate certain things.

When dating, do not put yourself in situations that make you uncomfortable. If a guy wants you to come to his house for dinner, but you barely know him or do not feel comfortable being alone with him, do not go. Some guys believe that if you are willing to come to their place alone, then you are willing to have sex. You may not be ready for that. Therefore, tell him to meet you in a public place. Tell him that you will drive to the location instead of him picking you up at your house. You want to know a person fairly well before letting him know where you live. They could have stalker tendencies. Stalkers are hard to get rid of I've heard.

With guarding your body comes protecting yourself when you decide you are ready to be sexual with a person. Diseases are rampant in our society. Not many people will tell you if they have a venereal disease that you could contract from them. They know that if they tell you, it is unlikely that you will stick around. So protect yourself until you become monogamous with your partner and you both have gone to check the status of your health.

Not only do you want to protect yourself from diseases, you also want to protect yourself from unplanned pregnancies. There are far too many single mothers raising children on their own because fathers run away from their responsibilities. Pregnancy is a beautiful thing when you do not have to go through it alone. Single-parent homes face many troubles that two-parent homes may not.

We talked about guarding your body; let's talk about guarding your heart. Do not give your heart to every man who comes along. Make a man earn your love. You should not be willing to give him everything from the start. My aunt used to say "Give him half of your heart." She explained it to me by saying, "Give a man half of your heart and see if he's going to put in the work to earn the other half." I did not understand this until I was in my late twenties. By then, my heart had been broken several times.

My heart was mostly broken because the guys I dated cheated on me. I believed that they loved me enough to only desire me and this simply was not true. Cheating is the ultimate betrayal for me. I feel that if I can demonstrate willpower by not cheating, my partner should be able to do so as well. I was giving more than I was receiving in those relationships and that was not healthy for me. I wrote a poem about it. Check it out.

One – Sided

Even a coin has two sides; you can flip it by
chance
But a coin has nothing to do with romance
Romance takes two people, a love story of
such
If the love is one-sided, then the love ain't
much
If I give one hundred percent of me, you give
eighty percent of you
Is that fair at all or what God intended for us
two?
I want to follow your lead, only if you're
taking God's path

'Cause him plus us has to be correct math.
There's never one side to a story, or one test
to take
Never one choice to pick or one decision to
make
Never one step left, or one battle to fight,
never one star that outshines the other on a
long cold night
But there may only be one chance of love
that's true
And when you find it, you treat it sacredly
like I plan to do
Because a love that's one-sided never lasts
for long
And it never really matters who's right or
wrong
Because if a rule is broken and one tries to
hide it
That equals a love lost because it was one-
sided

Chapter 13

Tired of Dating

If you feel as though you are tired of dating, you probably have been hurt numerous times and are just tired of starting relationships and them not ending in marriage. Take a step back and re-evaluate your relationships with men. Think about all of the things you could have done better or things that you should have done instead. Do not be afraid to learn from your mistakes.

When I realized that I was tired of dating, I also realized that I was ready for marriage. I did not wake up one day and decide that I wanted a husband. I prayed, cried and decided that I would wait for the special guy who was also ready for me. I stopped wasting time with guys with whom I knew I did not or could not have a serious relationship.

Chapter 14

The One

You have been dating this guy for a year or so and you want more, you say? If you think he is "the one," then you better make sure that he thinks the same of you. How can you tell if a man thinks you are the one he wants to spend the rest of his life with? He will tell you without you even asking him. He will show you in his everyday actions. He will take steps towards making that come true. It is up to you to decide how long you will date someone. I have several aunts who have never gotten married, but they have been with the same guy for more than a decade. I never understood why they cheated themselves out of getting the title of wife, but I promised myself that would never be me. I would never date a man for ten years or more. My limit is two. You have to figure out what your number is. If a man wants to make you his wife, it should not take him several years to do so. He can at least propose-with a ring-and you two work on the wedding plans. Men know what they want and how they feel about you. Communication is key. If you are not on the same page, then all you are doing is wasting valuable time.

Do not give a guy an ultimatum saying "If you do not propose to me by the end of the year, I am leaving." You do not have to threaten men into doing anything. If you feel as if you have been waiting too long for a commitment and you have spoken to your significant other about it several times, then just leave. Giving him an ultimatum will not change things. If he does not wish to marry you, then he will not marry you. He will continue to string you along as much as he can. He will continue to make promises that he never intends to keep. He will keep playing on your heart strings to make you stay knowing that he just wants to keep you around for his own benefit. Remember, you have the power. Use it! Do not give it away.

"The one" will usually act as such. He will want to be around you frequently. He will introduce you to his parents. He will take you out and buy you nice gifts. He will take interest in your everyday life. If you have children, he will try to get them to like him. If he is not the right guy for you, he will blow you off often, make excuses as to why you cannot meet his family and forget that it is your birthday; he won't even care if he meets your kids or not. There are certain behaviors that people display if they are truly interested in you. This goes for men and women.

Chapter 15

Different Kinds of Dating

Dating At Work

I advise you to avoid dating at work. Your place of employment is not an environment conducive to dating. Staying professional and tending to a relationship at the same time is extremely difficult. Plus, it could interfere with your daily duties and with the responsibilities of the job. Below are some of the reasons I am opposed to dating at work:

1. **It is hard to separate personal and working relationships.** If you and your significant other are mad at each other, it shows when you go to work. This is especially true if you work in the same area, usually go to lunch together, etc. You do not want everyone to know when you two are at odds with each other.

2. **There will be more people meddling in your business.** You already have to deal with family members and friends trying

to find out what is going on in your relationship, and now you have added coworkers. Some people are naturally nosy. They feed on gossip, drama and other people's business. Relationships are supposed to be private. It is impossible to keep your relationship private in a workplace.

3. **You do not have time to miss each other.** No matter how much you love your significant other, you need time away from them. Without time apart, you could feel smothered. Remember the phrase "Absence makes the heart grow fonder?" Often times, that phrase is true.

4. **If the two of you break up, you still have to see him.** In the past, when I've broken up with certain people, I did not want to see them ever again. Unless you quit, you're going to have to see this person frequently. The hope is that the two of you will remain cordial.

Dating at work, like any other circumstance, is not all bad. I am sure that there are benefits to working with someone you are dating. I would just advise you to approach the situation carefully and know what you are getting yourself into. Make sure that you and the person you are dealing with have a clear understanding of how you will conduct yourselves at work.

Online Dating

Online dating is prominent in today's society. Some people use it because they do not have a lot of time to date. Some people use it because they live in a small town and feel like they need to broaden their dating radius. Other people use it simply to try something new. Personally, I believe that most people try online dating out of desperation. They feel as though they have exhausted all other measures, so they turn to the internet. It gives them a glimmer of hope that they will not be alone forever.

Is Online Dating a Bad Idea?

Some women want to know if dating online is a bad idea. I believe that it works for some and it does not work for others. You should be your own judge and jury. There are several websites where you can try online dating-simply do a search on the internet to find them.

Maybe I am old fashioned, but to me, online dating is too impersonal. I prefer face-to- face interaction. I want to be able to look into someone's eyes when they are talking to me. I want to be able to feel if they are genuine in their feelings by watching their actions. I want to be able to pick up on certain characteristics such as chivalry, politeness and aggressiveness when on a date. If you are dating online, then you do not have those opportunities. Plus, with online dating, you do not know what the person actually looks like. Most people send you pictures of them that look nothing like them when you see them in person. I want to know what I am dealing with upfront. In general, with both online dating and regular dating, people will tell you anything. It is important to ask your potential partner a ton of questions. Usually, if it doesn't sound right, it most likely is not true.

In addition to dating on dating websites, you could potentially find partners on social media websites as well. These websites help you share personal things about yourself, show you things about other people and open you up to scores of people to whom you may take a liking. Plus, you are able to join for free. With the dating websites, some are free and others are not.

Long Distance Relationships

The truth about long-distance relationships is that they are more challenging than other relationships. Distance tests your relationship to the max. It can make or break it. If you start off in a long-distance relationship, eventually one of you will have to move to where the other person is for it to continue.

Dating long distance can be tricky. You have to have a high level of trust for each other for it to be successful. I do not trust people much, so long-distance dating did not work for me. I am one of those women that needs to be able to drive by your house to see if there are extra cars in the driveway. Don't judge me.

Teenagers Dating

My daughter is of age to date. One thing that I want for her is for her to be well-informed on relationships. I want her to know how she should expect to be treated, that it is okay to terminate a relationship if she is unhappy and that certain things are just unacceptable altogether. I want her to know about sexually transmitted diseases and about the options she has if she were ever to become pregnant. Some people believe that kids already know these things because they watch television or because their friends have told them. However, I do not want my daughter to rely on any information from either of those sources. They are unreliable and do not tell the entire truth. I have been having "the talk" with my daughter since she was around ten years old. She became inquisitive around that age, so I gave her as much information as I thought she needed to know. As she grew older,

I gave her more information as I saw fit. Now that she is a teenager, I believe that she is well-equipped with the information she needs.

Abstinence

By definition of Wikipedia, abstinence is "a voluntary restraint from indulging in bodily activities that are widely experienced as giving pleasure." Abstinence requires willpower. I tell my daughter to practice abstinence until she is married. I tell her to make sure that a man is worthy of her before giving him a gift that is so precious that can never be taken back. If you are about to marry someone, you are saying that they are worthy of all of you.

Now, I am all for teaching kids to abstain from sex, but how can we teach our children to practice abstinence in a world that believes that "sex sells?" You cannot turn around without being subjected to some form of it. It is on television, on the radio, in magazines and on the internet. It is extremely difficult to advise a teenager to abstain from sex when it is happening all around them. I tell my daughter to abstain from sex until she has a husband, but in this day and age, I believe that is very unrealistic. Teenagers think they are invincible and that nothing will happen to them if they subject themselves to danger. They believe that sex is just that and that there are no consequences; therefore, we have to equip them with knowledge. They are going to make their own decisions no matter how much we try to influence them. We can only hope, pray and watch them carefully to help them make good decisions.

If you do not know how to talk with your teenager about relationships, reflect back on your own life. Think about some of the mistakes you made while you were dating. Think about some of the things you did well. Think about the relationships that made you the happiest and those that made you miserable. Share some of those stories with your teenager. They may act like they are not listening, but they will remember what you shared later on.

Teenagers and Committed Relationships

Teenagers need to know that seriously dating in high school is not a smart idea. It is okay to have a few friends to hang out with at games and such, but attempting to have a lifelong committed relationship as a teenager is not wise. When you are young, you are supposed to explore the world, people and situations. You should not try to find a husband at sixteen years old. How can you find a lifelong mate when you do not completely understand who you are as an adult yet? Most teenagers cannot provide for themselves, they do not own their own car to drive around or know what career path they want to follow after high school. You cannot seriously date someone when this is the case. Now, I have seen people date in high school and end up married, but they are the minority. Also, just because high school sweethearts marry, that doesn't mean that they were ready or that they married the person who was designed for them.

Chapter 16

Enjoy Single Life

What do single people do? Whatever they want! They have no one to answer to, no one to cook for and no one to consider when they wish to spontaneously go out of town. Singledom is the life! Enjoy it while you can. Take trips with your girlfriends, party all night and flirt with as many guys as you want. There are several advantages to being single. A few of them being: there is no arguing or fighting with a mate, you don't have to buy gifts on holidays or birthdays (you can spend all of your money on yourself) and you can go out with whomever whenever you want. Being single means being free. You have liberties that committed people do not. I hope it does not sound like I am telling you to be wild, but that is EXACTLY what I am telling you to do (responsibly of course). If you are in college, act like it! If you are in your 20's, act accordingly. You have plenty of time to find your mate, settle down and have children. When you are single, you should enjoy being wild and crazy.

If I could relive my single days, there are many things that I would do before getting married. I would finish college, check a few more things off of my bucket list, take many more trips and probably enjoy the night life a little more. You can still do these things when you are married (except the night life part), but it is undoubtedly much harder. Finding balance in a marriage without losing yourself is a very hard thing to accomplish. I urge unattached women to enjoy everything while they can: themselves, their freedom, their kids, their social life, etc. Singledom and married life are two totally different universes. Marriage ties you down a great deal and out of respect for your spouse, there are things that you just shouldn't do anymore.

Once you have settled down, it is no longer all about you. It becomes about the two of you together. Are you ready for that? If you're under the age of twenty five, then probably not.

Worksheet

1. What are some things I would like to accomplish before marriage?

2. What are some things I believe would be better accomplished during marriage?

Chapter 17

The Breakup

Most relationships have a limited time span, so breaking up is something you are going to have to experience. The best way for you to do this is to have an adult conversation about why it is happening and then move on from one another. The worst way to break up with someone is by causing harm to them or their property. That particular way is also illegal. Learn to control your emotions early on. If you are in control of your emotions, then you will be able to handle situations such as a break up rather smoothly.

After a break-up, we tend to hold onto feelings for guys who we know are not right for us. Doing this only makes a bad relationship linger. I have seen individuals make up several times only to end up hating each other. Think about why you are doing what are you doing. Are you hanging on to him until you find someone new? You cannot find someone new while allowing him to continue to take up space at your house whenever you feel lonely. Get out and mingle instead. You two broke up for a reason. Just remember what that reason is so you won't double back.

Breaking up is not always a bad thing. For example, your relationship may have been abusive; getting out of that situation may have saved your life. Your relationship may have been mentally draining and removing yourself from it may have given you your vitality back. Whatever the reason, just be glad it happened and that it is over. Staying in an unhealthy relationship is not a smart move.

How to get over a breakup

Since I have broken up with a few people in my lifetime, I have figured out the best ways to get over them. I am not saying that it is a quick process, but in due time, you will no longer miss them or desire to call them. Take a look at the list below and see if some of these work for you:

1. **Have a pity party.** Watching a movie, eating ice cream and feeling sorry for yourself-whether alone or with your closest girlfriends-is ok to do. You are allowed to sulk for a little while because your relationship did not work out. The feelings that you have for someone does not go away overnight, but the pity party should only last for that long.

2. **Cry.** This can be done on the day of the break up or at the pity party, maybe even both. Crying does not mean that you are

weak. It means that you are upset and sad about a situation. Crying releases all of the emotions that you have bottled up inside. It is healthy. I'd rather you let it out by crying than by seeking revenge.

3. **Go to church.** This ALWAYS makes me feel better. I do not really have to explain this one, but go to places that make you happy. This could be church, the mall, the spa or a museum. Wherever your happy place is, go. It will take your mind off of things.

4. **Stay busy.** This is a very effective method of getting over a breakup. If you keep your mind busy with a task, then you have very little time to think about the negative things going on in your life.

5. **Spend time with someone else.** Men usually take this approach after a breakup. It works because you definitely do not have time to think about an ex if you are already hanging with someone else. However, do not rush into another relationship before you have completely gotten over your previous one. Hopping from one relationship to the next is not emotionally healthy.

Chapter 18

The Engagement

Let's say that your relationship did not fail and has evolved into engagement- Congratulations! My prayer for all of you who wish to be joined in matrimony is that you saying yes means that you are ready to spend the rest of your life with your current partner and that him proposing means that he is ready as well. Becoming engaged is the next step in the relationship and undoubtedly the most exciting. You are finally off the market and it feels wonderful. Your family and friends will celebrate with you and you will feel like you are on top of the world. However, just because you're engaged does not mean that the battle is over. The two of you are still dating, just in a different capacity. You have set a date to marry, but you still have to make it to the altar. Some couples become engaged and do not make it down the aisle for one reason or another. Be sure to continue to do what you were doing to make him propose and keep all of your relationship troubles between the two of you. Sometimes, family and friends can come between a relationship and cause it to fail. It is recommended that couples attend pre-marital counseling with the pastor whom they've chosen to facilitate their wedding.

Pre-marital counseling helps open your eyes to what the future holds for the two of you as husband and wife. It is a good idea to go in with questions that you want answered from an unbiased source.

Conclusion

I have talked about steps to take while preparing to be in a happy and fulfilling relationship. These steps are simply a guide to help you along your journey. Understanding what works for you and what does not will help you identify the type of mate that you wish to marry. Take heed to all of the information in this book as it is all tried and true. Peace and blessings to you!

About the Author

Theresa is a thirty-seven-year-old married Air Force veteran and mother. She has been a writer since the age of ten and recently decided to use her skills to help others in various areas of their lives. She enjoys traveling the world, mentoring and empowering people to be the best that they can be wherever they are in life.

She believes that everyone on Earth has a purpose and that fulfilling that purpose is the greatest pleasure one could ever experience. She uses her creativeness to give back to the people closest to her and to others around the world.

Worksheet

1. What character traits do I want to see in a potential mate?

2. What character traits in a potential mate are deal breakers?

3. What do I believe I did wrong in my last relationship?

4. What did I do right in my last relationship?

5. Am I insecure in my relationships? If so, why? Is it fair to be that way with someone who has not caused it?

6. Have I discussed the important topics with my current mate (kids, finances, unhealthy habits, religion, etc.)?

7. Who were/are my role models when it comes to healthy, happy relationships?

8. How long am I willing to date someone before exiting a relationship because of non-proposal?

9. Do I want my daughter/niece/grand-daughter to follow in my footsteps as it relates to how I allow men to treat me? Why or why not?

10. Who are the non-judgmental supporters in my life?

11. List three physical features you love about yourself.

12. List three character traits that you love about yourself.

13. When dating, am I the cause for the breakup? Why or why not? If so, have I gotten that issue under control?

14. Do I see a future with my current mate?

15. After reading this book, what are some things that I need to work on concerning my dating life?

Notes

Made in the USA
Middletown, DE
23 December 2020

30032241R00046